Learning & Caring About

OUR TOWN

Compiled by Elizabeth McKinnon

Illustrated by Barb Tourtillotte

Warren Publishing House, Inc.
Everett, Washington

Editorial Staff:
>Gayle Bittinger, Kathleen Cubley, Brenda Mann Harrison, Jean Warren, Erica West

Design and Production Staff:
>*Production Manager:* Jo Anna Brock
>*Art Director:* Jill Lustig
>*Cover Illustration:* Kathy Kotomaimoce
>*Cover Design:* Eric Stovall
>*Book Design:* Sarah Ness

Copyright © 1992 by Warren Publishing House, Inc. All rights reserved. Except for reproducing the parent-flyer pages for non-commercial use or including brief quotations in a review, no part of this book may be reproduced in any form without the written consent of the publisher.

ISBN 0-911019-54-5

Library of Congress Catalog Card Number 92-80995
Printed in the United States of America
Published by: Warren Publishing House, Inc.
>P.O. Box 2250
>Everett, WA 98203

20 19 18 17 16 15 14 13 12 11 10 9 8 7 6 5 4 3 2

Introduction

Our Town is designed to help teachers and parents introduce young children to their community and some of its workers.

The book is filled with easy, hands-on activity suggestions for art, language, learning games, music, movement and snacks. All of the activities are developmentally appropriate for young children and use materials that are readily available.

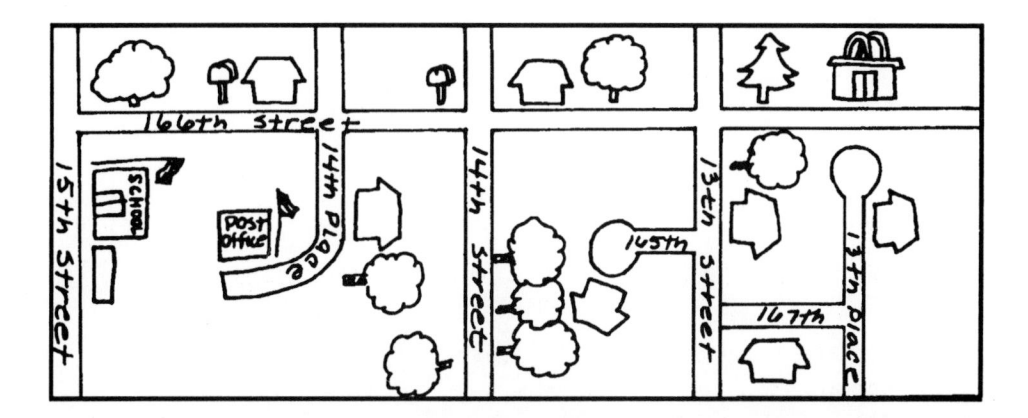

Our Town's first chapter explores places where people live and caring for the community. The second chapter centers around familiar community helpers such as the police officer, the firefighter and the mail carrier. Also included are sections on traffic safety and fire safety. The last chapter covers several of the public places found in towns — the library, the zoo, the school and the park.

Each chapter in the book is followed by reproducible parent flyers. The flyers suggest activities that parents can do with their children to reinforce their understanding of concepts covered in the chapters.

Young children are naturally curious about the world around them. By building on this curiosity and using the activities in *Our Town* as springboards, you can help your children begin to discover what makes their community a special place.

Elizabeth McKinnon

Contents

Where We Live
Houses and Homes 8
All Around Town 12
Caring for the Community 16
Parent Flyers 20

Community Helpers
Police Officer 24
Traffic Safety 28
Firefighter 34
Fire Safety 40
Doctor/Nurse 42
Dentist 46
Mail Carrier 50
Veterinarian 54
Parent Flyers 58

Some Places We Go
Getting There 66
Library 68
Zoo 70
School 72
Park 74
Parent Flyers 76

Learning About

WHERE WE LIVE

Houses and Homes

Collage of Homes

Hang a piece of butcher paper on a wall at the children's eye level. Title the paper "Places People Live." Have the children look through magazines and newspapers to find pictures of different kinds of homes (houses, apartments, condominiums, trailers, houseboats, tents, etc.). Let them tear or cut out the pictures and glue them to the butcher paper any way they wish to create a group collage. Encourage the children to talk about the different kinds of homes pictured in their collage as they are working.

Variation: Let younger children choose from precut pictures of homes that have been placed in a box.

Shoebox Dollhouses

Give each child a shoebox to use for making a dollhouse. Have the children stand their boxes on one side as shown in the illustration. Let them decorate the walls of their houses by gluing on pieces of wallpaper or patterned wrapping paper. Have them color the floors with crayons or let them attach construction paper "carpets." Help the children cut pictures of furniture and people out of store catalogs. Glue the pictures to empty thread spools to make them stand properly. Then let the children have fun arranging the furniture in different ways and playing house with their dollhouse people.

Variation: Have each child decorate the inside of a shoebox to represent an apartment. Then stack the boxes and fasten them together with tape or glue to create an apartment house.

Houses and Homes

Homes

Ask one child at a time to tell where he or she lives (in a house, an apartment, a mobile home, etc.). Then recite the following poem for the child, substituting his or her name for *Matthew* and a description of where he or she lives for *in a house*.

A squirrel lives in a tree,
    (Make tree shape with hands.)
A snail lives in a shell.
    (Cover fist with opposite hand.)
A bear lives in a cave,
    (Make fist with thumb inside.)
It suits her very well.

A fish lives in a fishbowl,
    (Make circle with hands.)
A bird lives in a nest.
    (Cup hands together.)
Matthew lives in a house,
    (Make roof above head with arms.)
He thinks his home is best.

Elizabeth McKinnon

Inside and Outside

For each child, fold a large piece of construction paper in half crosswise. Then cut the paper into a house shape, as shown in the illustration, with the fold as the top of the roof. Cut pictures from magazines of items that are found inside a house (furniture, appliances, curtains, etc.) and items that are found outside a house (trees, cars, garbage cans, etc.). Set out the pictures along with containers of glue. Let the children select pictures, decide if the items belong inside or outside and then glue the pictures on the insides or outsides of their house shapes.

Where We Live

Houses and Homes

Finger Puppet Fun

For each child, use a paper plate to make a finger puppet theater. Cut a horizontal slit in the plate as indicated in the illustration. Cover the edges of the slit with tape to prevent paper cuts. Make a 1-inch vertical cut at each end of the slit. Let the child use crayons or felt-tip markers to draw a picture of his or her home on the plate. Help the child write his or her address on or above the picture. With a washable felt-tip marker, draw a face on one of the child's fingers to create a finger puppet. Have the child insert the puppet through the back of the slit in the puppet theater and act out stories about living in his or her home.

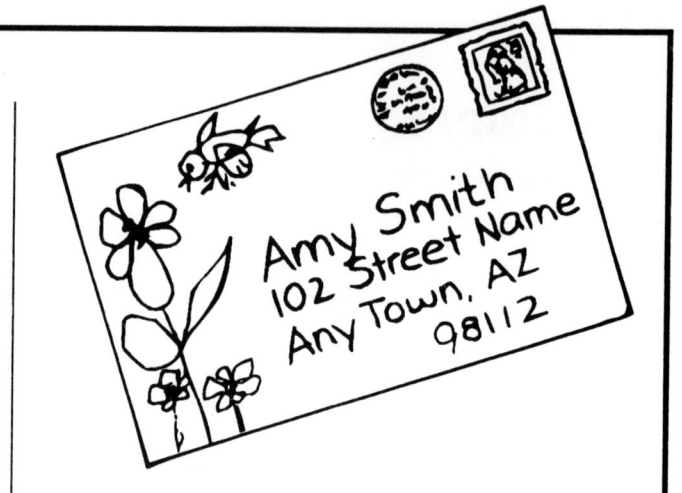

I Know My Address!

Encourage the children to learn their own addresses by doing the following activities.

- Play games in which the children must say their addresses. For example, have them pretend to order pizzas to be delivered to their homes. Or have them pretend to be lost and tell a "police officer" where they live.

- Write each child's address on a separate piece of paper and cover it with clear self-stick paper. Let the child trace over his or her address with a finger or a crayon while saying the address aloud. (Have the child erase the crayon marks by rubbing them with a dry facial tissue.)

- When a child has learned to say his or her address, write it on a plain postcard (or a large index card) that the child has decorated. Add a short note, if desired. Then mail the card so that the child will receive it at home as a special acknowledgment.

Where We Live

Houses and Homes

Building a House
Sung to: "Twinkle, Twinkle, Little Star"

Building a house is lots of work,
First, you dig up lots of dirt.
    (Pretend to dig.)
Next, you pour a concrete floor,
    (Touch floor.)
Put up boards and pound nails galore.
    (Pretend to hammer.)
Finally, the house is finished,
    (Clasp both hands together.)
And people are ready to live in it.

Diane Thom

Mini-House Sandwiches

Let the children help make Mini-House Sandwiches for snacktime. To make four sandwiches, cut the crusts off two slices of bread and spread on peanut butter. Cut one slice into four squares and the other slice into four triangles. Have the children arrange the bread squares on plates and place a bread triangle "roof" above each square. Let them decorate their house sandwiches with sunflower seeds, raisins or shredded coconut, if desired.

Where We Live

All Around Town

Play Town Map

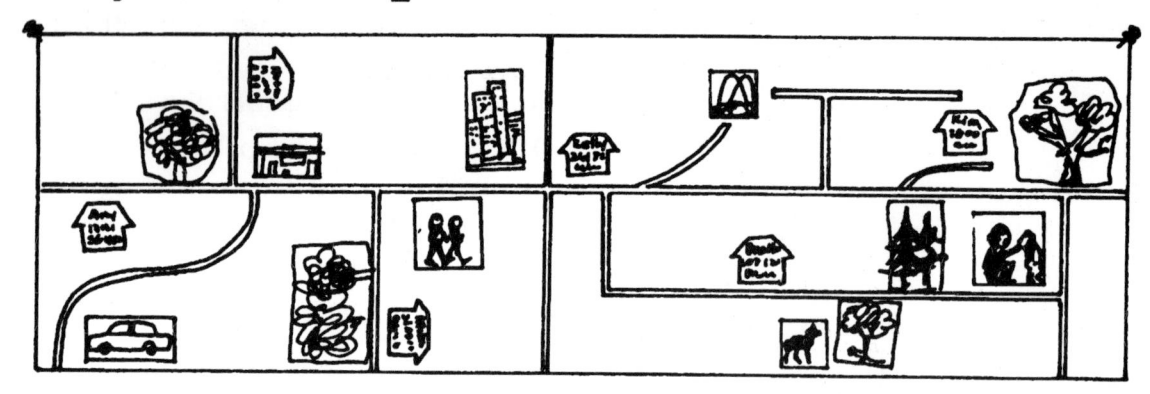

Draw a map that includes roads and grassy areas on a long piece of butcher paper. Let the children help color the map with crayons or felt-tip markers. Hang the map on a wall at the children's eye level. Give each child a house shape cut from construction paper to decorate and attach to the map. (Write the children's addresses on their house shapes, if desired.) Then set out a box containing pictures of stores and other buildings, cars, trees, people and pets. Let the children choose pictures and add them to the map.

Variation: Let the children help paint a road map on butcher paper that has been attached to a tabletop or the floor. Have them make houses and other buildings to stand on their map by decorating small boxes or milk cartons. To make standing trees, cut slits in the ends of toilet tissue tubes and insert green construction-paper foliage shapes. As your play town grows, encourage the children to think of new things to add such as a blue paper river or a gray paper parking lot marked with stalls for toy cars.

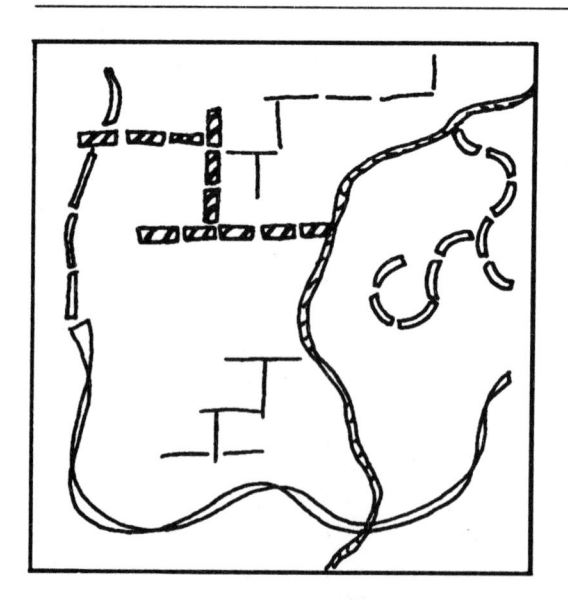

Road Collages

Give each child a large piece of construction paper. Set out glue and containers of straight and curvy materials such as yarn pieces, plastic straw segments, toothpicks, ribbon pieces and uncooked pasta noodles. Let the children glue lines of the different materials on their papers to create "roads." Encourage them to fill their papers with straight roads, winding roads and roads that intersect.

Where We Live

All Around Town

Itty Bitty City

Display picture postcards or other kinds of photographs of your downtown area. Have any of the children ever been downtown? If so, encourage them to tell about the different kinds of buildings they saw. Then set out pieces of plywood or flat boards and an assortment of scrap wood pieces. (Check local lumber companies for free or inexpensive wood scraps.) Let the children work together to create their own city by gluing the wood pieces together any way they wish.

Variation: Let each child create his or her own city.

Community Map

Use several yards of bolt felt to make a map of your community that includes the area in which your children live. Use craft paints or felt-tip markers to draw on and label streets. Draw or glue on felt shapes to represent familiar landmarks such as stores or restaurants. Also add mailboxes, trees and similar items as desired. Give each child his or her own house shape cut from felt. Let the children have fun arranging and rearranging their house shapes on the map. As they do so, encourage them to say their addresses.

Variation: Make the map out of a piece of denim and use pieces of Velcro for attaching the house shapes.

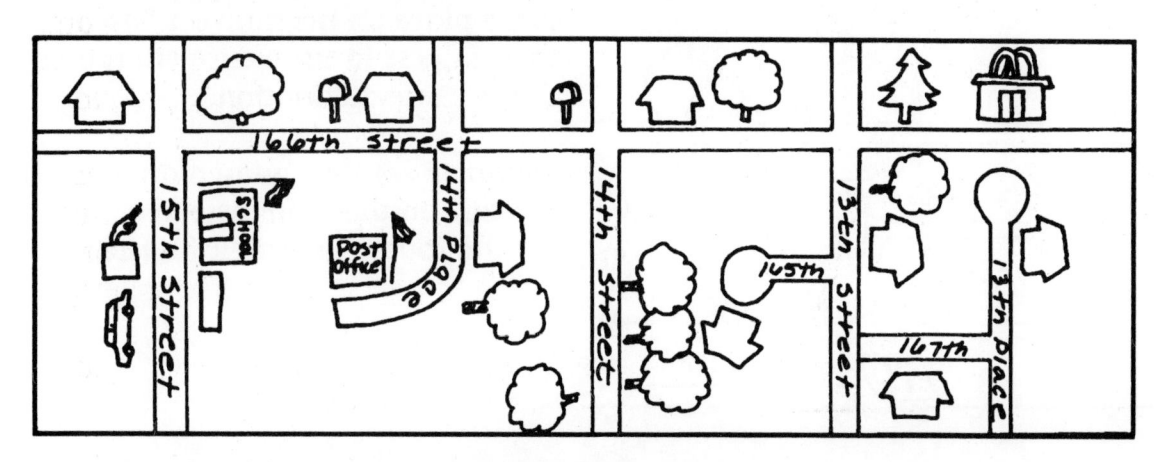

Where We Live

All Around Town

Road and Car Match

Tape a piece of butcher paper to the floor. Draw red, yellow and blue roads on the paper using felt-tip markers or crayons. Set out red, yellow and blue toy cars. Let the children select cars and drive them on the matching colored roads.

Variation: Make roads on the floor with pieces of red, yellow and blue plastic tape.

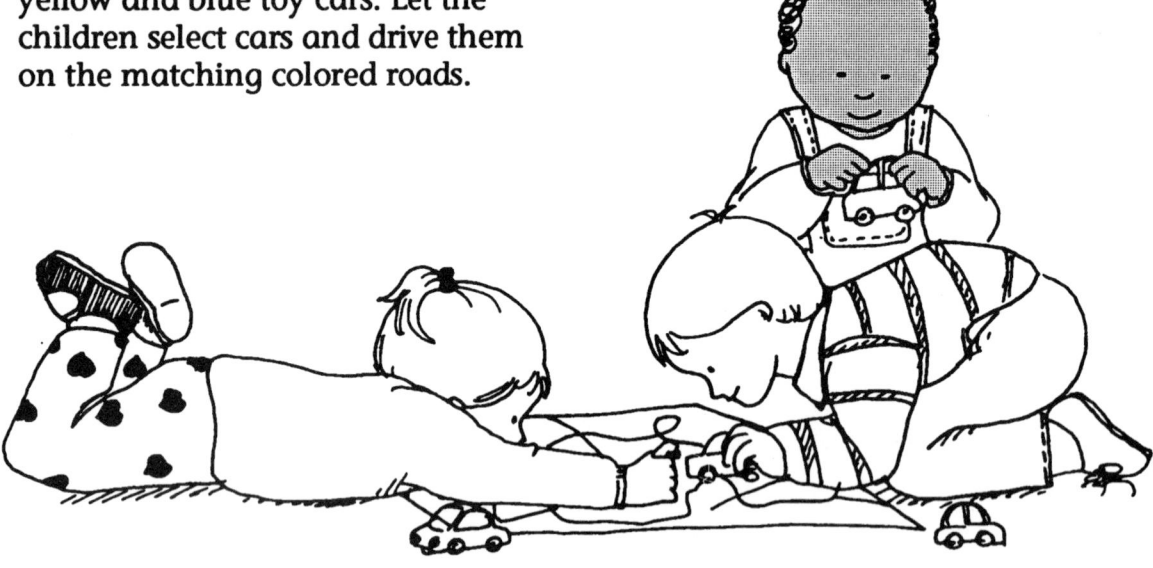

How Can We Get There?

Draw a map of a play town on a large piece of posterboard or cardboard. Include intersecting roads, a park, several houses, a grocery store, a gas station, etc. Cover the map with clear self-stick paper. Let several children at a time start at the same place on the map and use their fingers to trace different routes to the same destination.

Variation: Let the children drive tiny toy cars on the map instead of tracing routes with their fingers.

Where We Live

City Sounds

Use a tape recorder to record familiar sounds heard in your neighborhood or community (a car horn, a jackhammer, a fire engine siren, a splashing fountain, a train whistle, etc.). Play the tape for the children and have them try to identify the different sounds.

Let's All Walk Down the Street
Sung to: "If You're Happy and You Know It"

Let's all walk down the street, down the street,
Let's all walk down the street, down the street.
Let's all walk down the street,
Smile at everyone we meet.
Let's all walk down the street, down the street.

Let's all ride down the street, down the street,
Let's all ride down the street, down the street.
Let's all ride down the street,
Wave at everyone we meet.
Let's all ride down the street, down the street.

Let's all drive down the street, down the street,
Let's all drive down the street, down the street.
Let's all drive down the street,
Honk at everyone we meet.
Let's all drive down the street, down the street.

Jean Warren

Caring for the Community

Room Helpers

Help the children learn how to do room tasks such as wiping off the art table, sweeping the floor, watering the plants or passing out snacks. Make a helper chart that includes photographs of the children doing the different tasks. Label spring-type clothespins with the children's names. At the beginning of each week, clip the clothespins next to the photographs on the chart. Let the children search for their names and look at the pictures to discover what their room tasks are for the week.

This Is the Way

At cleanup time, help the children understand that working together can make the job easier for everyone. To reinforce the spirit of cooperation, sing the following song, substituting the name of the task at hand for *pick up the toys*.

Sung to: "The Mulberry Bush"

This is the way we pick up the toys,
Pick up the toys, pick up the toys.
This is the way we pick up the toys,
So early in the morning.

Deb Cech

Where We Live

Caring for the Community

Play Yard Beautification

Help the children develop a sense of pride about making their play yard an attractive place in the neighborhood. Several times a week, take them outside to pick up paper and other trash that has collected around the yard. If desired, let the children help decide on special projects such as planting a tree seedling for Arbor Day or decorating a shrub with bird treats for the winter holidays.

Trash Song

Sung to: "London Bridge"

Trash is blowing all around,
All around, all around.
Trash is blowing all around,
All around the town.

Let's get busy and pick it up,
Pick it up, pick it up.
Let's get busy and pick it up,
All around the town.

Put the trash in a big trash bag,
Big trash bag, big trash bag.
Put the trash in a big trash bag,
All around the town.

Carol Mellott

Where We Live

Caring for the Community

Planting Flowers

For a springtime science project, let the children plant marigold or other flower seeds in containers filled with potting soil. Have them place the containers in a sunny spot and add water regularly. When the seedlings are several inches tall, let the children help transplant them outside to beautify your play yard. Once the flowers are in bloom, have the children work together to weed and water their garden.

Variation: Have each child grow several flowers in separate cups. Let the children take their flowers home to give to neighbors for planting outdoors.

Greeting Card Fun

Help the children learn to think about and care for others by encouraging them to make different kinds of greeting cards. For example, let them make a card for a sick classmate by decorating a long piece of paper on which you have written "Get well soon." Roll up the paper and deliver it to the recipient. Or have the children decorate folded pieces of construction paper to make friendship cards and deliver them to a nearby children's hospital or nursing home. When appropriate, have the children make thank-you cards to send to community helpers or to people who have done special things for your group.

18   Where We Live

Caring for the Community

Helping Hands Books

Talk with the children about tasks they could do at home to help their families. Then let them make Helping Hands Books to give as gifts. Trace around each child's hand on several sheets of paper. Cut out the hand shapes to make pages and let the child decorate them as desired. Fasten each child's hand shapes together to make a book. Attach a note to each book explaining that the recipient can tear out a page and present it to the child when a helping hand is needed.

White Elephant Sale

Have a White Elephant Sale to raise money for a local food bank, children's shelter or other charity that you and your children wish to help. Ask the children and their parents to bring in items in good condition that they no longer use. Have the children help you sort the items, set up displays, make signs and sell the items. After the sale, let the children participate when the money is actually given to the chosen charity.

Extension: If any items remain after the sale, donate them to a local charity. Use your White Elephant Sale to help the children see how items can be reused, or recycled, and how waste can be reduced in your community.

Where We Live

Parent Flyer

Dear Parents,

We have been learning about where we live. Try doing the following activities to help your child discover some things about your home and neighborhood.

My Own Home

Cut a large house shape out of construction paper that matches the color of your own home. Give your child light-colored paper squares to glue on the house shape for windows. When the glue has dried, let your child draw faces of family members and pets on the window squares. Help your child mount the house shape on a large piece of paper and write your address on it. Let your child add grass, trees and other decorations as desired. Then display the house picture in your child's room to help him or her remember your address.

Around the Block
Sung to: "Frere Jacques"

Let's go walking, let's go walking,
Around the block, around the block.
We will keep on walking,
We will keep on walking,
Then we'll stop, then we'll stop.

Additional verses: Let's go skipping; hopping; riding; driving.

Jean Warren

Address Labels

If you have printed address labels, give several to your child as a "prize" when he or she has learned to say your address correctly. Or make address labels for your child to attach to toys or other objects. Use a permanent felt-tip marker to print your child's name and your address on removable self-stick labels or strips of masking tape.

Map Fun

With your child, make a simple floor map of his or her room. Include symbols to represent things such as the door, the bed and the rug. Have your child wait while you hide a small treasure in the room and mark its position on the map with an X. Then let your child use the map to discover the hidden treasure.

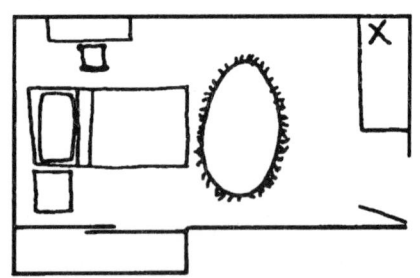

Extension: Gradually make simple maps of larger areas such as your home, your yard and your neighborhood. As you explore these areas with your child, work together to add special details to your maps.

Copyright ©1992 Warren Publishing House, Inc. All rights reserved.
Parent Flyer may be reproduced for noncommercial use.

Parent Flyer

Dear Parents,

We have been learning about caring for our community. Try doing the following activities to help your child discover ways of helping out in the place where you live.

I Want to Be a Helper
Sung to: "Did You Ever See a Lassie?"

I want to be a helper,
A helper, a helper.
I want to be a helper,
I will help Mommy this way.
I will pick up my toys,
I will pick up my toys.
I want to be a helper,
I will help Mommy this way.

I want to be a helper,
A helper, a helper.
I want to be a helper,
I will help Daddy this way.
I will rake up the leaves,
I will rake up the leaves.
I want to be a helper,
I will help Daddy this way.

Encourage your child to sing about other ways of helping Mommy or Daddy.

Sandra E. Fisher
Susan A. Miller

Caring and Sharing

Do one or more of the following activities with your child.

- Set out a large box for reusable items such as empty egg cartons, plastic foam food trays and rinsed-out juice cans. Donate the items to your child's play group.

- When you go to the supermarket, buy a nonperishable food item to donate to your local food bank.

- Let your child choose a toy or game to donate to a local children's shelter.

- Save recyclable items such as old newspapers, aluminum cans and glass jars. Let your child help take them to a local recycling center or sort and bag them for curbside recycling.

- Have a Cleanup Day about once every month. Take trash bags outside and walk around your yard and neighborhood, picking up litter. Plan a special treat to enjoy with your child when you have finished.

- Let your child make a cheery greeting card to send to a shut-in friend or relative.

Copyright ©1992 Warren Publishing House, Inc. All rights reserved.
Parent Flyer may be reproduced for noncommercial use.

Where We Live Contributors

Ideas in this chapter were contributed by:

Janice Bodenstedt, Jackson, MI
Deb Chech, Mt. Penn, PA
Sandra E. Fisher, Kutztown, PA
Rita Galloway, Harlingen, TX
Joan Hunter, Elbridge, NY
Carol Mellott, Superior, NE
Susan A. Miller, Kutztown, PA
Beverly Qualheim, Marquette, MI
Diane Thom, Maple Valley, WA
Kristine Wagoner, Puyallup, WA

Learning About

COMMUNITY HELPERS

Police Officer

Police Cars

Set out cardboard cartons (large enough to stand in) with the tops and bottoms removed. Let the children turn the cartons into police cars by brushing on blue and white paint. Add yellow paper-plate headlights and black paper-plate wheels. If desired, glue red and blue glitter above the cars' headlights to represent flashing lights. Make a set of suspenders for each carton by attaching two pieces of heavy yarn from front to back. Have the children stand inside the cartons and place the suspenders over their shoulders. Then let them "drive" their police cars around the room.

Variation: Instead of using yarn suspenders, cut holes for handles in the sides of the cartons.

Police Badges

For each child, cut a 5-inch star shape out of lightweight cardboard and a slightly larger star shape out of heavy-duty aluminum foil. Show the children how to fold the edges of their foil shapes around their cardboard shapes to make silver stars. Tape the loose edges to the backs of the stars, if necessary. Cut a 3-inch circle for each child from gray construction paper. Use a black felt-tip marker to write "Police" and a numeral of the child's choice on it. Let the children glue their circles in the centers of their foil stars. Complete the badges by taping safety pins to the backs of the stars.

Community Helpers

I'm a Police Officer
Sung to: "I'm a Little Teapot"

I'm a police officer
With my star,
I help people
Near and far.
If you have a problem,
Call on me,
And I will be there
One, two, three!

Judy Hall

The Traffic Cop Song
Sung to: "Do Your Ears Hang Low?"

Do you drive a car
With a flashing light on top?
When you hold up your hand,
Does the traffic have to stop?
Can you blow a whistle loud,
Standing straight and tall and proud?
You're our friend, the traffic cop.

Diane Thom

Police Officer

Police Officer Dramatic Play

Let the children take turns being police officers for the following activities.

- Have officers pretend to direct traffic and tell others how to cross the street.

- Let officers hand out "tickets" for breaking rules and good citizen awards for doing nice things for others.

- Make pretend driver's licenses for the children to carry when using riding toys. If a child is stopped by an officer for not following established safety rules, have the child turn in his or her license for the day.

- Let officers pretend to take lost children home after the children have stated their names and addresses. Or have the children tell the officers their home telephone numbers to call on a play phone.

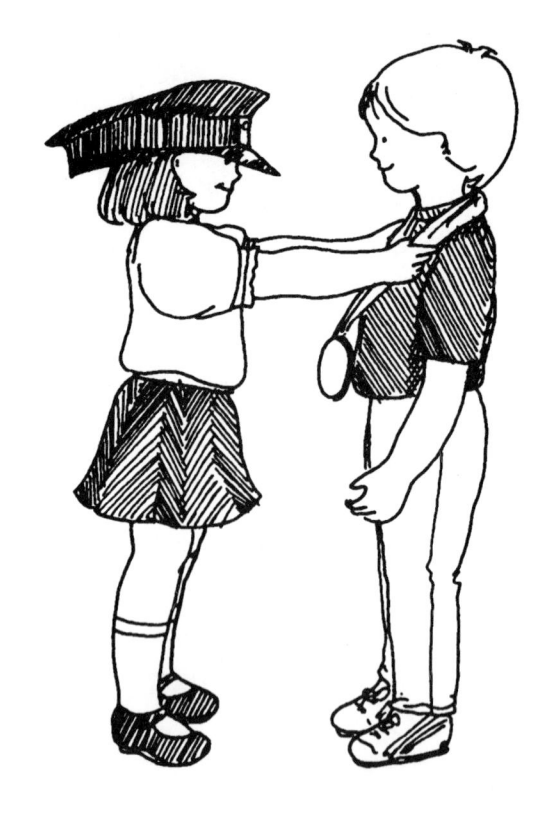

- Discuss the 911 emergency telephone number and when it is appropriate to dial it. Let the children practice dialing the 911 number on a play phone, reporting emergencies and giving their addresses so that officers can respond.

9-1-1

Sung to: "Three Blind Mice"

9-1-1, 9-1-1,
Help's on the way, help's on the way.
If I need help, I know what to do,
I can call the police and the firehouse, too,
It makes me feel safe to know what to do.
Dial 9-1-1.

Sue Brown

26 Community Helpers

Police Officer

Police Officer Visit

Invite a police officer to visit your group. Arrange for the officer to show and discuss tools of the trade such as a police uniform, a hat, a badge, an identification card and a two-way radio. Ask the visitor to talk with the children about how the police officer is their friend. If desired, ask the officer to discuss safety rules such as obeying traffic signs and not talking to strangers. If observing a police car is part of the presentation, be aware that the sound of the siren can be frightening for some children.

Variation: Ask the visiting officer to come dressed in street clothes and then change into uniform. (This will help the children understand that a police officer is an ordinary person who wears a uniform at work.)

Who Is Lost?

Have the children sit with you in a group. Choose one child to be the Police Officer. Tell the officer that you are looking for a lost child. Then describe one of the other children by giving clues such as these: "He is a boy. He has black hair and brown eyes. He is wearing a yellow shirt." Have the Police Officer look around the group, identify the lost child and bring the child to you. Continue the game, each time choosing different players.

Community Helpers

Traffic Safety

Double Stops

For each child, cut an 8-inch stop sign shape from red construction paper. Print "STOP" on both sides of each shape. Have the children trace over the letters on one side of their stop signs with glue and sprinkle on silver glitter. When the glue has dried, have the children repeat the process on the opposite sides of their stop signs. Staple each sign to a paper towel tube. Let the children use their signs for playing stop-and-go games.

Stop, Look and Listen

Help the children learn the following poem. Encourage them to recite it whenever they come to a street crossing.

Stop, look and listen
Before you cross the street.
First use your eyes and ears,
Then use your feet.

Traditional

Traffic Safety

Before You Cross the Street

Sung to: "London Bridge"

Look before you cross the street,
Cross the street, cross the street.
Look before you cross the street.
Do be careful!

If the light is red, don't go,
Red, don't go; red, don't go.
If the light is red, don't go.
Do be careful!

Wait until the light is green,
Light is green, light is green.
Wait until the light is green.
Do be careful!

Look before you cross the street,
Cross the street, cross the street.
Look before you cross the street.
Do be careful!

Judith Taylor Burtchet

Traffic Light Game

Make a traffic light by covering a half-gallon milk carton with black construction paper and letting the children help glue on red, yellow and green construction-paper circles. Discuss what the three colors mean. Then hold up the traffic light and let the children move around the room, pretending to drive cars. When you call out "Green," have them go. When you call out "Yellow," have them slow down. When you call out "Red," have them stop. Continue the game, letting the children take turns calling out the colors.

Community Helpers

Traffic Safety

The Traffic Light
Sung to: "If You're Happy and You Know It"

When you see the light is green, it means go.
When the light is yellow, caution — please go slow.
You must stop if it is red,
Yes, that is what I said.
Now you know when to stop, slow down and go.

Diane Thom

Traffic Signs Book

Make a book containing pictures of different kinds of traffic signs that the children can see in your area. For example, you might include pictures of a stop sign, a slow sign, a walk sign, a do-not-walk sign, a do-not-enter sign, a one-way street sign, a yield sign and a speed-limit sign. Read the book to the children at circle time. Then place it in your book corner where the children can enjoy "reading" it by themselves.

Hint: Check a driver's manual for pictures of traffic signs that are used in your state.

Community Helpers

Traffic Safety

Steering Wheels

For each child, cut a paper plate into a steering wheel shape as shown in the illustration. Let the children personalize their steering wheels by decorating them with crayons, felt-tip markers or paints.

Extension: Have the children hold their steering wheels and pretend to drive cars as you sing the following song. Each time you come to the end of the song, have the children stop their cars.

Sung to: "Ring Around the Rosie"

See the green light glowing,
See the traffic flowing.
Yellow light,
Red light,
Traffic, stop!

Bobby Lee Wagman

Traffic Light Snacks

Give each child a half of a hot dog bun. Let the children spread on mayonnaise, if desired. Set out red pepperoni circles, yellow cheese circles and green pickle circles. Let the children create "traffic lights" by arranging the red, yellow and green circles in vertical rows on their hot dog buns.

Community Helpers

Traffic Safety

Seatbelt Play

Purchase used seatbelts from a local junkyard. Shorten them as necessary with scissors. Then use a hot glue gun to attach the seatbelts to several child-size chairs in your room. (Make sure that each seatbelt is just large enough to fit across a child's lap when fastened.) Let the children have fun lining up the chairs to make cars. Have them buckle up before they start to "drive."

Variation: Use pieces of wide elastic with magnets attached to the ends for seatbelts.

Do You Always Wear Your Seatbelt?

Sung to: "Have You Ever Seen a Lassie?"

Do you always wear your seatbelt,
Your seatbelt, your seatbelt,
Do you always wear your seatbelt
When you ride in the car?

Does Ashley?
   (Child responds.)
Does Cody?
   (Child responds.)
Does Joseph?
   (Child responds.)
Does Katie?
   (Child responds.)
Oh, we always wear our seatbelts
When we ride in the car.

Substitute the names of your children for *Ashley*, *Cody*, *Joseph* and *Katie*. Continue singing the song until each child's name has been mentioned.

Frank Dally

Car Safety Song

Have the children sit in chairs and pretend to be car passengers. Talk about why it is important to fasten seatbelts and to sit quietly when riding in a car. Then sing the following song.

Sung to: "Do Your Ears Hang Low?"

When you ride in the car,
Going near or going far,
Are you buckled in your seat?
    (Pretend to fasten seatbelt.)
Well, that's really neat!
Do you sit quietly,
    (Fold hands in lap.)
Looking at the scenery,
    (Look left and right.)
When you ride in the car?
YES!

Diane Thom

Car Ride

Sung to: "Twinkle, Twinkle, Little Star"

To go near or to go far,
You can ride inside a car.
Give your seatbelt a good click,
Now, that ought to do the trick.
It's good to know you're safe and sound
When you're riding all around.

Diane Thom

Firefighter

Firefighter Hats

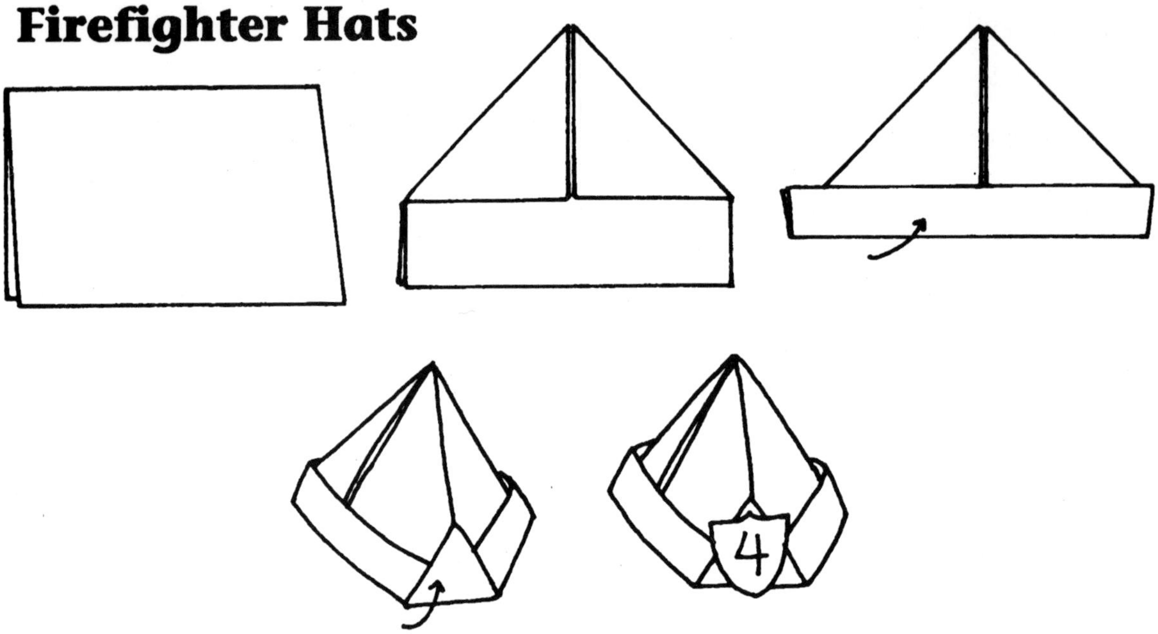

For each child, use plain newsprint (or newspaper) to make a folded paper hat. Secure all loose edges with tape. Let the children use crayons or felt-tip markers to color their hats red. Fold back one corner of each hat and staple it in place. Then attach a yellow construction-paper badge shape on which you have written a numeral of the child's choice.

Variation: For each child, trim a large piece of red construction paper into an oval shape. Then use the oval to make a head-size version of the firefighter finger puppet hat described on page 38.

I'm a Firefighter
Sung to: "I'm a Little Teapot"

I'm a firefighter
Dressed in red,
With my fire hat
On my head.
I can drive the fire truck,
Fight fires, too,
And help to make things
Safe for you.

Judy Hall

Community Helpers

Fire Station Play Center

Set up an area of the room to represent a fire station. Supply it with fire station items such as firefighter hats, boots, jackets, gloves, pails, flashlights, a rope, a hose, a toy fire truck, a bell and a sleeping bag. Let the children pretend to be firefighters staying at the fire station. Encourage them to jump out of bed when the fire bell rings, get dressed quickly and then drive out in their fire truck to fight the fire.

Down at the Firehouse

Sung to: "Down by the Station"

Down at the firehouse
Early in the morning,
You can see our clothes
Hanging in a row.
When there is a fire,
We can dress real fast.
Boots, jackets, hats, gloves,
Off we go!

Jean Warren

Firefighter

Firefighter Visit

Invite a firefighter to come and talk with the children. Ask the visitor to bring his or her special clothing and gear, including air tank and gas mask. Arrange for the firefighter to put on the clothing and gear as the children watch. An appropriate topic for the firefighter to discuss would be the importance of not playing with matches or lighters. If the visiting firefighter comes in a fire truck, keep in mind that the sound of the siren can be frightening for some children.

Cardboard Carton Fire Engine

Select a rectangular cardboard carton, like the one in the illustration, to use for making a fire engine. Cut the bottom out of the carton with a craft knife. Open out the two long top flaps. Cut square holes in them as shown to make the flaps into "ladders." Let the children paint the ladders white and the rest of the carton red. When the paint has dried, attach two small yellow paper plates for headlights and four large black paper plates for wheels. Cut holes for handles in the front and the back of the fire engine. Add a section of garden hose to hang out the back hole. Let the children take turns climbing inside the fire engine and driving it to imaginary fire scenes.

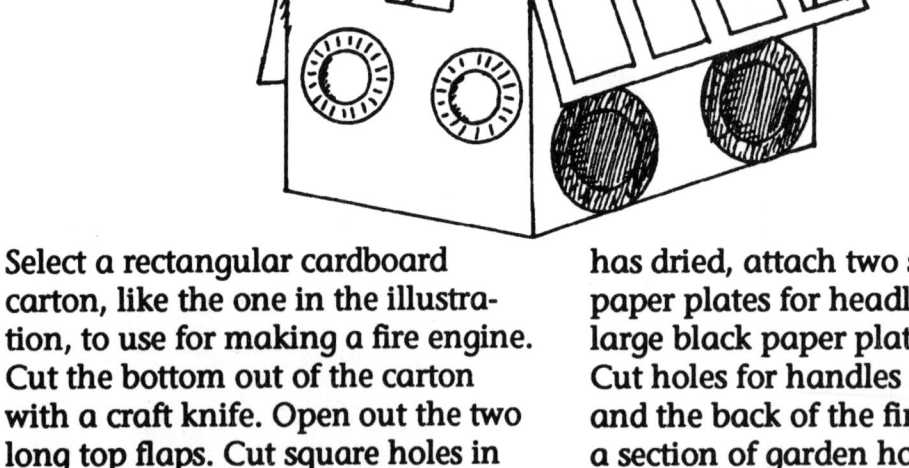

Community Helpers

Fire Truck Scenes

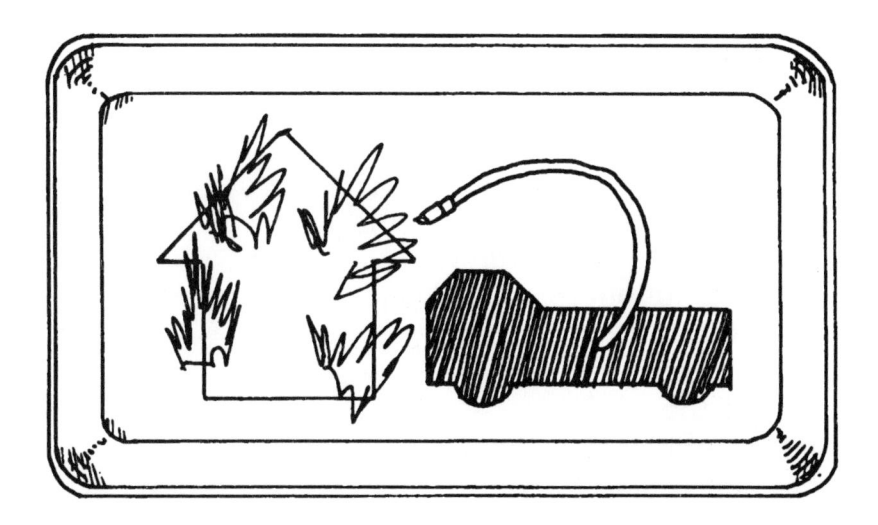

Help the children make Fire Truck Scenes. For each scene, give a child a small house shape and a fire truck shape cut from construction paper. Let the child glue his or her shapes on a plastic foam food tray. When the glue has dried, have the child use felt-tip markers to draw smoke and flames coming out of the house. Make a hose for the fire truck by wrapping a small piece of masking tape around one end of a pipe cleaner. Poke the other end through the fire truck shape and secure it with tape to the back of the tray. Let the child wiggle the hose and pretend to put out the fire in the house.

Big Red Fire Truck
Sung to: "Twinkle, Twinkle, Little Star"

Big red fire truck, ladder on top,
Going to a fire where it will stop.
Long curving hose carried about,
Splashing water from its spout.
The fire and smoke are going away,
Now it's time to shout "Hurray!"

Substitute *yellow* for *red*, if appropriate for your area.

Diane Thom

Firefighter

Firefighter Finger Puppets

Let each of the children make one or more firefighter finger puppet hats. For each hat, give a child an oval shape (about 2 inches long) cut from white construction paper. Let the child use a crayon to color both sides of the oval red. Cut out a finger hole, as indicated by the dotted line in the illustration, and fold as indicated by the solid line. Use a black felt-tip marker to add a numeral of the child's choice to the hat. Draw a face on the child's finger as shown and top the finger with the child's firefighter hat.

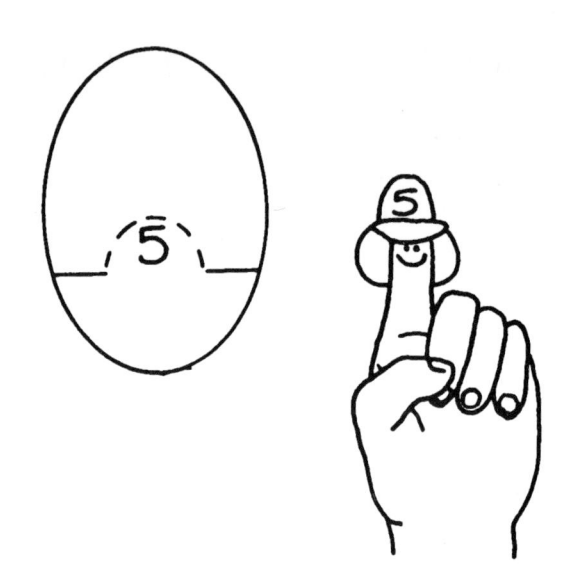

Encourage the children to manipulate their puppets while singing songs or telling stories.

Five Friendly Firefighters

Five friendly firefighters standing near the door,
One washes the fire engine, now there are four.

Four friendly firefighters waiting patiently,
One fixes the hoses, now there are three.

Three friendly firefighters have a lot to do,
One climbs up a ladder, now there are two.

Two friendly firefighters exercise and run,
One cooks some dinner, now there is one.

One friendly firefighter — all the work is done,
This one goes to bed, now there are none.

Diane Thom

Community Helpers

Firefighter

Firefighter Training

Let the children pretend to train for becoming firefighters. Lay a 6-foot ladder flat on the floor. As you hold on to the ladder, have the children try doing these activities: step between the rungs without touching the sides; walk just on the sides of the ladder; walk just on the rungs; jump back and forth over the ladder. Then stand the ladder on its side and let the children try tossing beanbags through the openings between the rungs.

To the Rescue!

Have the children put on their firefighter hats from the activity on page 34. Let them help you stand a short ladder against a cupboard. Hold on to the ladder while the children take turns climbing it to rescue a small doll which you have placed on top of the "burning building."

Note: Make sure the children understand that they should never play on a ladder unless an adult is present and that actual fire rescues are jobs for real firefighters.

Community Helpers

Fire Safety

Fire Safety Bulletin Board

Talk with the children about fire safety rules: don't play with matches or lighters; don't play with electrical cords or sockets; keep away from things that are hot; etc. Make a chart of the rules and hang it on a bulletin board. Let the children use red, yellow and orange paints to create fire pictures on pieces of black construction paper. Arrange the pictures around your fire safety chart to complete your bulletin board display.

We Do What Sparky Says

Display a picture of Sparky the Fire Dog (check your local fire department for materials about Sparky). Then sing the following song with the children.

Sung to: "Ten Little Indians"

We are friends of Sparky the Fire Dog,
We are friends of Sparky the Fire Dog,
We are friends of Sparky the Fire Dog,
We do what Sparky says.

Sparky says don't play with matches,
Sparky says don't play with matches,
Sparky says don't play with matches,
We do what Sparky says.

Additional verses: Sparky says don't play with lighters; Sparky says don't play with hot things.

Elizabeth McKinnon

Fire Safety

Fire Prevention Badges

Cut badge shapes out of white index cards. Let the children decorate their badges with orange and yellow felt-tip markers. Use a black felt-tip marker to write these words on each child's badge: "(Child's name) does not play with matches or lighters." Then tape a safety pin to the back of the badge and pin it to the child's shirt.

Stop, Drop and Roll

Each time you have a fire drill, talk with the children about how they should "Stop, Drop and Roll" if their clothes catch on fire. Clear a large area in the room or take the children outside to a grassy area. Have the children start walking or running in place. At a given signal, have them stop what they are doing, drop to the floor or ground and roll over and over until the pretend flames are out.

Doctor/Nurse

Doctor/Nurse Bags

For each child, use a folded piece of black construction paper to make a "doctor's bag." With the fold as the bottom of the bag, round off the top corners with scissors. Cut two handle shapes from black construction paper and attach them to the top of the bag as shown in the illustration. Give the children their bags along with one each of several medical items such as tongue depressors, cotton balls, adhesive bandages and cotton swabs. Let the children glue or tape their items inside their bags. Have them attach self-stick dots for pills, if desired. When the glue has dried, let the children use their bags for dramatic play.

I'm Happy I'm a Doctor
Sung to: "My Bonnie Lies Over the Ocean"

I'm happy I'm a doctor,
I help to make people well.
I'm happy I'm a doctor,
It makes me feel just swell.
I'm a doctor,
I help to make people well, well, well.
I'm a doctor,
I'm happy, can't you tell?

Jean Warren

Doctor/Nurse

I'm a Nurse Dressed in White

Sung to: "Little White Duck"

I'm a nurse dressed in white,
And I feel just swell.
When you are sick,
I help to make you well.
I give you shots,
And if you're afraid,
I fix you up with a big Band-Aid.
I'm a nurse dressed in white,
And I feel just swell.
Now you're well!

Jean Warren

Bandages for "Ouches"

Set out large pieces of construction paper and paints, crayons or felt-tip markers. Let the children draw pictures of themselves with two or three "ouches" on their bodies. Then give them adhesive bandages to attach to their pictures. (Use bandages that have colorful patterns, if available.) As the children are working, encourage them to talk about shots, hurts or falls they have experienced. What did they do to help their "ouches" feel better?

Community Helpers

Doctor/Nurse

Doctor/Nurse Visit

Invite a doctor or a nurse to visit your group. Ask your visitor to bring several medical instruments such as a stethoscope, a reflex hammer and a light for looking into eyes and ears. Ask your visitor to talk about caring for cuts and bruises, practicing healthy habits and similar issues. If possible, arrange for the nurse or doctor to bring disposable face masks (or other disposable items) to hand out to the children.

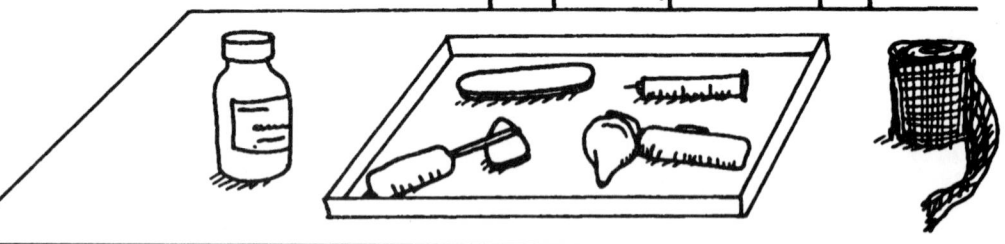

Good Health Story

Collect a variety of items that promote good health such as a comb, a bar of soap, a facial tissue, an apple, a jump rope and a small pillow. Place the items in a large bag. Have the children sit with you in a circle. Start telling a "good health" story about a child or an animal character. Then let the children take turns removing items from the bag and holding them up. As each item is displayed, incorporate it into your story. Continue until all the items have been used.

Community Helpers

Doctor/Nurse

Doctor's Office Play Center

Set up a doctor's office in a corner of your room. Supply it with medical items such as white jackets, doctor bags, pretend prescription pads, a stethoscope, a bathroom scale, an eye chart, tongue depressors, bandages, cotton balls and cotton swabs. Let the children take turns being doctors\nurses and patients. Encourage them to take pulses, give pretend shots, listen to hearts, bandage arms and legs, write pretend prescriptions and give out healthy advice ("Get plenty of rest. Drink lots of orange juice. Exercise every day.")

Good Health Posters

Let the children help make Good Health Posters to display around the room or in your Doctor's Office Play Center. For example, on a large piece of construction paper, draw or glue a picture that illustrates washing hands. Add the title "Wash Hands." Let the children decorate the poster by gluing on soap bar wrappers. Other poster ideas include using facial tissue (decorate with real tissues), eating nutritious foods (decorate with canned fruit and vegetable labels), exercising regularly (decorate with pictures of outdoor play) and keeping hands off dangerous substances (decorate with Mr. Yuk stickers.)

Community Helpers

Dentist

Toothy Smiles

Set out bowls of white navy beans. Give each child a smiling lips shape (about 3 by 6 inches) cut from red construction paper. Squeeze a horizontal band of glue across the center of each lips shape. Then let the children place the white beans on the glue to represent teeth.

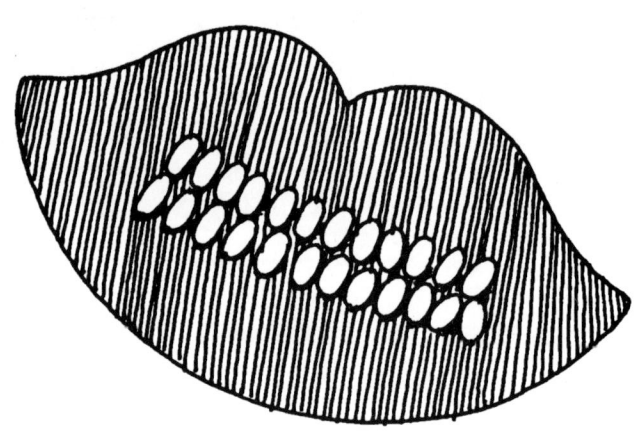

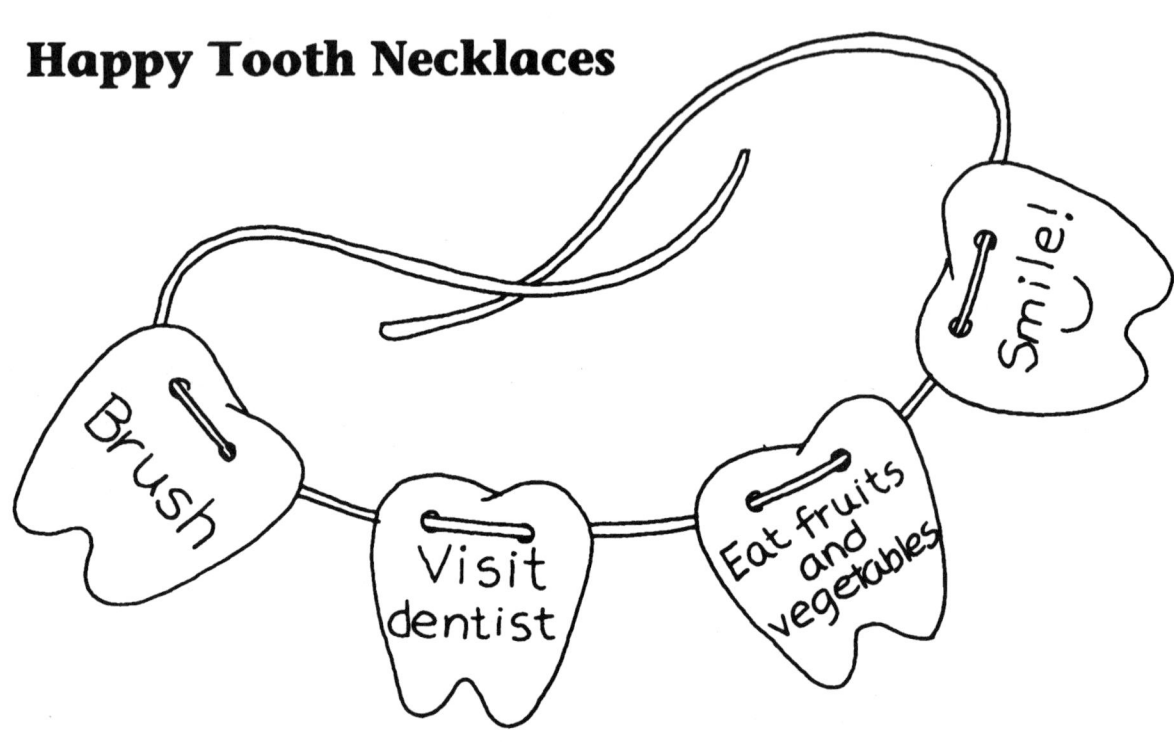

Happy Tooth Necklaces

Give each child several tooth shapes cut from white construction paper. Help the children decorate their shapes with pictures or words that express "happy tooth" messages such as these: "Brush. Visit dentist. Eat fruits and vegetables. Smile."

Punch two holes at the top of each tooth shape. Let the children string their shapes on pieces of yarn, as shown in the illustration. Tie the ends of each child's yarn piece together and help the children put on their necklaces.

Community Helpers

Dentist Visit

Invite a dentist or other dental care worker to visit your group. Ask your visitor to bring a tooth model, a toothbrush and dental floss to use for demonstrating the proper way to brush and floss teeth. You might also ask your visitor to bring a few small dental instruments such as a pick and a mirror. Arrange for your visitor to talk with the children about how teeth grow and about the kinds of foods they should eat to keep their teeth and gums healthy.

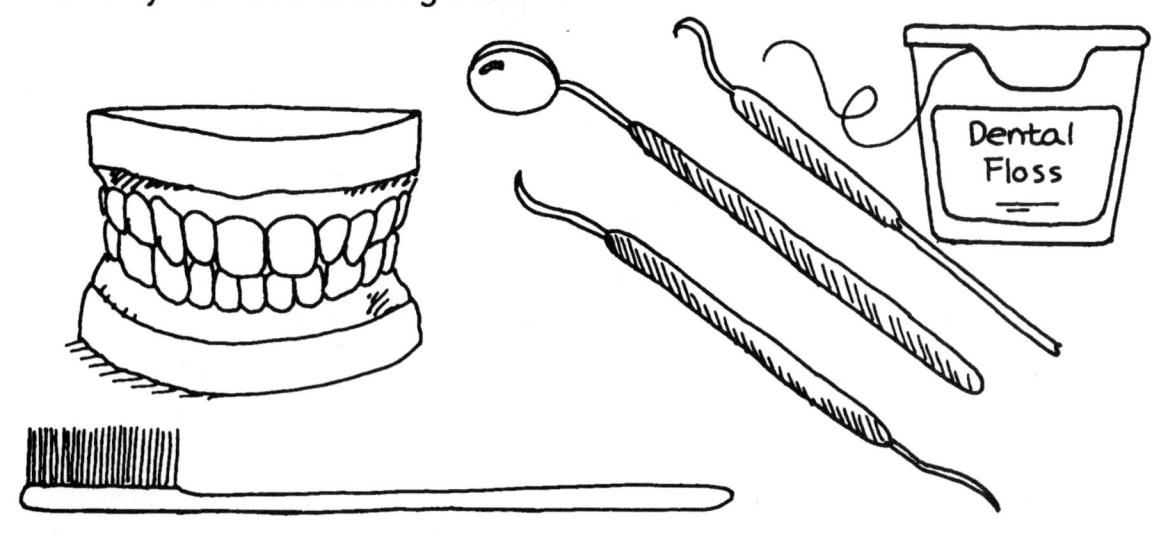

Dr. Denise the Dentist

Sung to: "Rudolph the Red-Nosed Reindeer"

Dr. Denise the Dentist
Helps me keep my teeth so white.
Dr. Denise the Dentist
Teaches me to brush just right.
Dr. Denise the Dentist
Always wears a super smile.
Dr. Denise the Dentist,
I'll be your friend a long, long while.

Substitute any other name for *Denise*.

Betty Silkunas

Community Helpers

Brushing Teeth

Talk with the children about the importance of brushing their teeth after eating meals and sugary snacks. Also discuss the proper way to use a toothbrush. Then make "mint toothpaste" by mixing green and white tempera paint together. Give each child an old toothbrush and a large tooth shape cut from white posterboard or cardboard. Let the children brush their tooth shapes with the green paint toothpaste. Encourage them to brush back and forth, up and down and in a circular motion. (Remind the children that the toothpaste is pretend and should not be put into their mouths.)

Do You Brush Your Teeth?

Sung to: "Do Your Ears Hang Low?"

Do you brush your teeth
After every meal you eat?
    (Pretend to brush teeth.)
Is your smile so bright
It shines like a light?
    (Smile and point to teeth.)
Do you open your mouth wide
So the dentist sees inside?
    (Open mouth wide.)
Do you brush your teeth?
    (Pretend to brush teeth.)

Diane Thom

Happy Tooth, Sad Tooth Poster

Divide a piece of butcher paper in half. Draw a smiling tooth at the top of one half and a frowning tooth at the top of the other half. Let the children glue magazine pictures of low-sugar snack foods (fresh fruits, raw vegetables, nuts, milk, etc.) on the "happy tooth" side of the butcher paper and pictures of high-sugar snack foods (candies, cookies, cakes, colas, etc.) on the "sad tooth" side. Display the finished poster on a wall or a bulletin board.

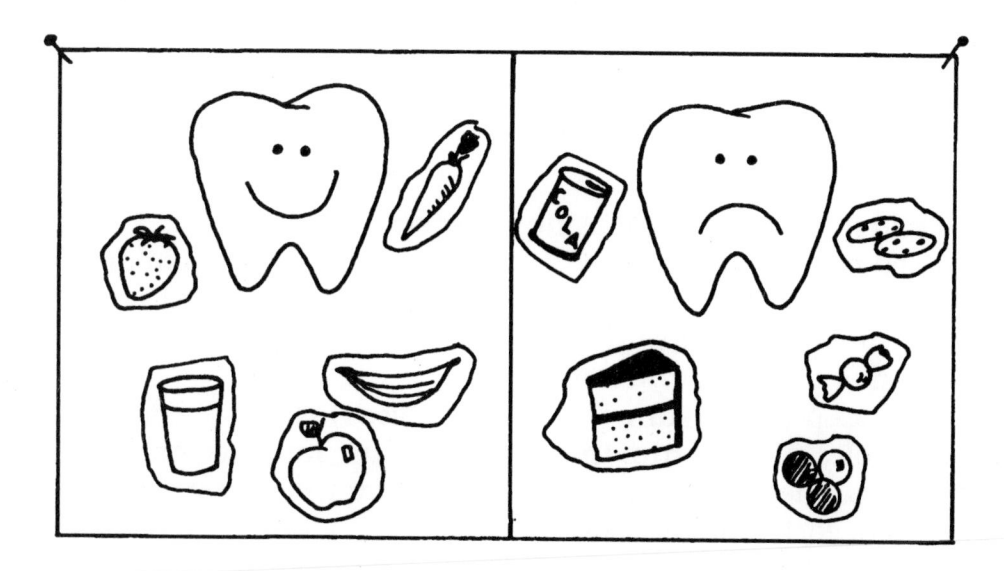

Happy Tooth Snacks

Discuss with the children how choosing low-sugar snacks, instead of those with lots of added sugar, can help prevent cavities. At snacktime, serve foods such as apple slices, carrot and celery sticks, or fresh strawberries with plain yogurt dip. Make sure the children understand that it is all right to eat some sugary foods, if they don't eat too many and if they brush after eating.

Mail Carrier

Mail Bags

Let each child make a mail bag using a large folded piece of brown construction paper. Use a hole punch to punch holes along the sides and the folded bottom of each bag and have the children lace pieces of yarn through the holes. Tie and trim the loose yarn ends. Then attach a long piece of yarn to each bag for a shoulder strap and write "U.S. Mail" on both sides. Give the children pieces of junk mail to place in their bags for "delivering."

Variation: Instead of construction paper, use large rectangles cut from heavy brown grocery bags.

Mail Carrier Song
Sung to: "My Bonnie Lies Over the Ocean"

I get to sort the mail,
Then carry it to your home.
The mail comes from all over,
Like New York, Paris and Rome.
Mail, mail, mail, mail,
I love to deliver the mail, mail, mail.
Mail, mail, mail, mail,
I love to deliver the mail.

Jean Warren

Community Helpers

Mail Carrier

Paper Bag Mailboxes

Let the children make "mailboxes" to use when handing out valentines or other kinds of cards they have made. Give them each a white paper craft bag (or lunch bag) placed flat on a table. Have them glue red and blue strips cut from construction paper across the tops and bottoms of their bags. In the center of each bag, write "Mail for (child's name)." At the top of the back side of each bag, use a brass paper fastener to attach a small flag shape cut from red construction paper. Let the children decorate the back sides of their bags with red and blue crayons, if desired.

When it's time to "deliver" the cards, stand the mailboxes on a table and let the children place their cards inside.

Post Office Play Center

Set up a play post office in a corner of your room. Supply it with items such as these: postal scales, play money, stamp-like stickers, junk mail, packages wrapped for mailing, a rubber date stamp and an ink pad. Let the children paint a cardboard carton blue to make a large mailbox for the post office. Then have them decorate and stack shoeboxes to use for sorting mail. Let the children take turns being the mail sorter and the stamp seller. Encourage the rest of the children to "write" letters to mail at your post office.

Community Helpers

Mail Carrier

Visiting the Post Office

Let each child make a greeting card for someone who lives in his or her home. After placing each card in a separate envelope, address it and let the child attach a postage stamp. (If desired, ask parents to contribute stamped envelopes.) Then take the children on a visit to your local post office to mail their cards. Arrange ahead of time for someone to guide you through the post office so that the children can see what happens to letters after they are dropped into the mail slot. Over the next few days, have the children watch for their cards to be delivered to their homes.

Variation: Let the children make cards for one another. Place all the cards in one large envelope. Address the envelope to your group at your teaching center. Mail the envelope on your visit to the post office. Then have the children keep an eye out for the mail carrier to deliver their special mail.

Mailbox Sorting Game

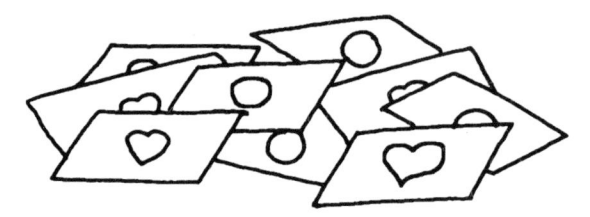

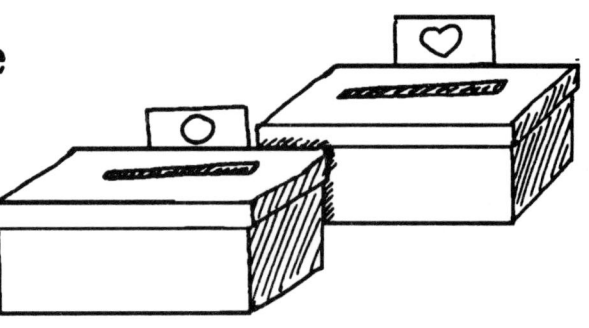

Make mailboxes by covering the lids of two or more shoeboxes with construction paper and cutting a slit in the top of each lid. Put the lids on the boxes. Draw different shapes (a circle, a heart, etc.) on small index cards. Tape the cards to the backs of the mailboxes so that they stand above the lids. Make pieces of mail for each mailbox by drawing a matching shape on the fronts of several sealed envelopes. Then mix up all the envelopes and let the children take turns mailing them through the slots of the appropriate mailboxes.

Variation: Mark the mailboxes and envelopes with matching colors, numerals or alphabet letters.

Community Helpers

Mail Carrier Movements

Let the children pretend to be mail carriers. Ask them to show how they would carry deliveries such as a bunch of letters, a package of feathers, a package containing skis or a package filled with books. Then let them pretend to deliver letters to people who live in different places (at the top of a tall apartment building, in the middle of a snowy field, on an island, at the North Pole, on the moon, etc.).

Do You Drive a Mail Truck?

Sung to: "Do Your Ears Hang Low?"

Do you drive a mail truck,
Walk in snow and rain and muck,
To deliver mail over hill and dale?
Do you carry great big boxes,
Heavy like they're filled with rocks?
Do you drive a mail truck?

Diane Thom

Veterinarian

Veterinarian Headbands

For each child, cut a 3- to 4-inch circle out of cardboard. Let the children cover their circles with aluminum foil. Staple each child's circle to a construction-paper headband. Then fit the headband around the child's forehead and fasten the ends together with staples or tape. Let the children wear their headbands when they examine stuffed animal "patients."

I'm a Vet

Sung to: "Oh, My Darling Clementine"

I'm a vet, I'm a vet,
I'm a veterinarian.
I take care of the animals,
And I treat them one by one.

I give shots, I set legs,
And sometimes I operate.
I take care of the animals,
'Cause I think they are just great.

Bring your dogs, bring your cats,
Bring your hamsters one by one.
I take care of the animals,
I'm a veterinarian.

Repeat, letting the children substitute other animal names for *dogs, cats* and *hamsters*.

Jean Warren

Community Helpers

Veterinarian

Vet's Office Play Center

Set up a pretend veterinarian's office in a corner of your room. Supply it with items such as an examination table, white jackets, strips of gauze, a stethoscope, cotton balls, cotton swabs, a brush and a comb. Let the children take turns being veterinarians and taking care of stuffed animals that the rest of the children bring in for treatment. Have the veterinarians give pretend shots, tie on bandages, demonstrate how the animals should be groomed and discuss good health rules for pets.

Vet's Office Mural

Cut pet animal shapes, such as cats, dogs, birds and bunnies, from different colors of construction paper. Let the children choose the shapes they want and glue on appropriate textured materials (yarn pieces on cat shapes, construction paper "spots" on dog shapes, feathers on bird shapes, cotton on bunny shapes, etc.). Use a black felt-tip marker to divide a piece of butcher paper into large squares. Hang the paper on a wall next to your Vet's Office Play Center. Then help the children attach their animal shapes to the butcher paper inside the square "cages."

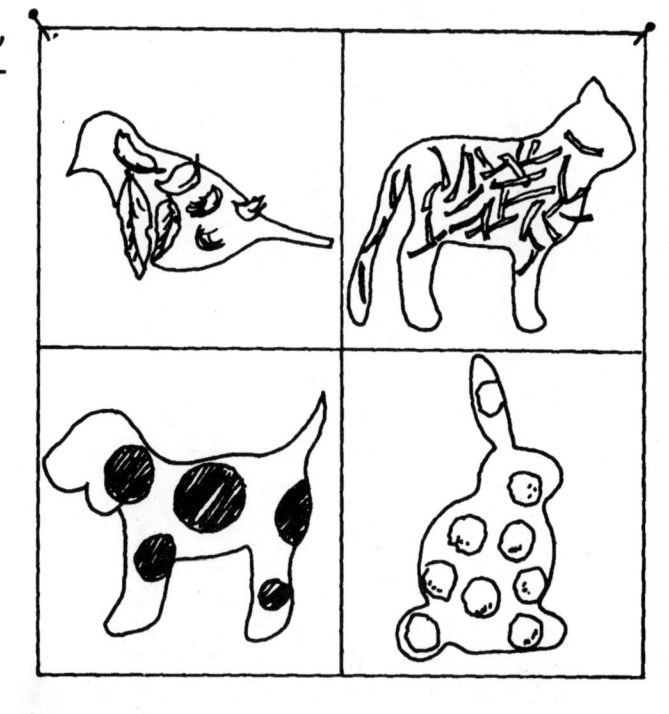

Community Helpers

Veterinarian

Veterinarian Visit

Invite a veterinarian or veterinary worker to visit. Arrange for him or her to bring a kitten or puppy to show to your group. Ask your visitor to show the children the proper way to hold and play with the animal. Have the visitor discuss pet care, including feeding, grooming, exercising and having regular checkups. If possible, arrange to have your visitor show the children some pet supplies such as a feeding dish, a collar and a few toys.

Pet Days

Allow each child to have a special Pet Day. On that day let the child bring in his or her pet for a short visit. (Make arrangements with parents in advance.) If a child does not have a real pet, have him or her bring in a toy pet.

Variation: If some children are unable to bring in their pets, let them share photographs of their pet animals on their Pet Days. Encourage them to tell how they care for their pets at home.

Community Helpers

Love Your Pets

Talk about the things pets need every day to keep healthy and strong such as food, water, exercise, rest and lots of love. Then sing the following song with the children.

Sung to: "Row, Row, Row Your Boat"

Love, love, love your pets,
Love them every day.
Give them food and water, too,
Then let them run and play.

Love, love, love your pets,
Love them every night.
Let them sleep till they wake up,
In the morning light.

Elizabeth McKinnon

What Kind of Vet?

Choose one child to be a zoo-animal vet, another child to be a farm-animal vet and a third child to be a house-pet vet. Set out pictures of different kinds of animals (or use toy animals). As you hold up each one, ask each vet to say whether or not he or she would treat that animal. When the proper vet has been decided upon, give the animal picture to that child. Continue playing the game until all the animals have been sorted. Then choose three new players to be vets and start the game again.

Parent Flyer

Dear Parents,

We are learning about community helpers. Try doing the following activities to reinforce your child's understanding of the police officer and traffic safety.

Police Officer Game

Pretend to be a police officer. Ask your child: "What is your name? Where do you live? What is your telephone number?" Then let your child be the police officer and ask you the questions.

I'm a Police Officer
Sung to: "The Muffin Man"

You can trust a police officer,
Police officer, police officer.
You can trust a police officer,
If you need some help.

I will keep you safe from harm,
Safe from harm, safe from harm.
I will keep you safe from harm,
I'm a police officer.

Jean Warren

This You Should Know
Sung to: "The Farmer in the Dell"

When you get in a car
And before it starts to go,
Always buckle your seatbelt.
This you should know.

The red traffic light means stop.
The green traffic light means go.
The yellow light means caution.
This you should know.

Betty Silkunas

My Telephone Book

Teach your child how to dial 911 (or 0) and the telephone numbers of relatives or friends who could help in an emergency. Write the numbers on separate index cards. Let your child glue a picture of a police officer on the 911 card and photos of relatives and friends on their corresponding telephone number cards. Laminate the cards, if desired. Then fasten them together with small metal rings to make a telephone book for your child. If desired, add a card with your child's photo and your complete phone number on it for the book's cover.

Copyright ©1992 Warren Publishing House, Inc. All rights reserved.
Parent Flyer may be reproduced for noncommercial use.

Parent Flyer

Dear Parents,

We are learning about community helpers. Try doing the following activities to help your child learn more about the firefighter and fire safety.

The Firefighter Song
Sung to: "Do Your Ears Hang Low?"

Do you put fires out
With a hose that has a spout?
    (Pretend to aim fire hose.)
Do you wear a special suit
With a fire hat and boots?
    (Touch head, then feet.)
Do you come immediately
When we dial 9-1-1?
    (Pretend to use telephone.)
Do you put fires out?
YES!

Diane Thom

Fire Drill

Make a plan for getting out of your home in case of fire and establish a safe place outside for everyone to meet. Practice following your plan with your child on a regular basis. At the end of your fire drill, have your child show how he or she would get help by pretending to run to a neighbor's house and dialing 911.

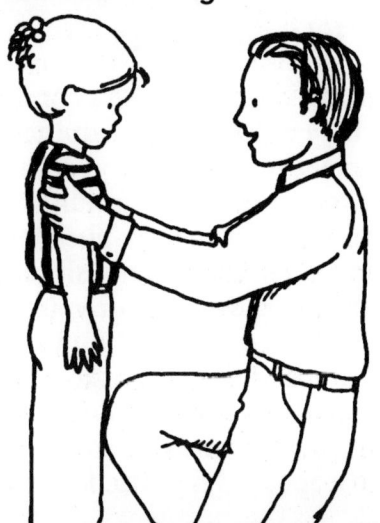

Never Play With Matches
Sung to: "Frere Jacques"

Never, never play with matches.
If you do, if you do,
You might burn your fingers,
You might burn your fingers.
That won't do! That won't do!

Never, never play with matches.
If you do, if you do,
You might burn your house down,
You might burn your house down.
That won't do! That won't do!

Repeat, substituting *lighters* for *matches*.

Leora Grecian

Copyright ©1992 Warren Publishing House, Inc. All rights reserved.
Parent Flyer may be reproduced for noncommercial use.

Parent Flyer

Dear Parents,

We are learning about community helpers. Try doing the following activities to help develop your child's understanding of the doctor and nurse and of good health practices.

Good Health Calendar

Make a calendar page for one week that includes a space for a picture. With your child, choose a good health habit to write on your calendar page such as "We eat healthy snacks." Let your child decorate the calendar as desired. At the end of each day, attach star stickers to your calendar to show that you and your child practiced your good health habit. Make a new calendar page each week for habits such as these: "We go to bed on time. We wash our hands before we eat. We get our exercise."

Going to the Doctor
Sung to: "She'll Be Coming Round the Mountain"

Going to the doctor, yes we are,
Going to the doctor, yes we are.
Be sure to take good care
Of our bodies inside there.
   (Point to self.)
Going to the doctor, yes we are.

Going to see the nurse, yes we are,
Going to see the nurse, yes we are.
Be sure to take good care
Of our bodies inside there.
   (Point to self.)
Going to see the nurse, yes we are.

Kristine Wagoner

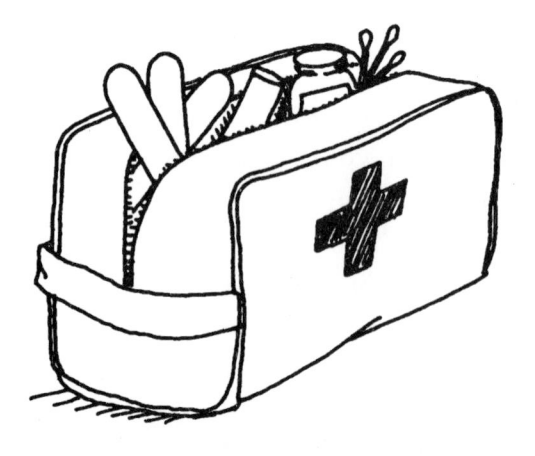

Let's Visit the Doctor

Make arrangements to take your child to your doctor's office for a "learning visit." Ask to have someone show you and your child around the office, introduce the doctor and nurse and answer any questions your child may have. After your visit, make a pretend doctor/nurse bag for your child to play with. Label an old shaving kit with a red cross made with plastic tape. Fill the bag with items such as bandages, tongue depressors, cotton swabs, small bottles, a toy stethoscope and a gauze face mask.

Copyright ©1992 Warren Publishing House, Inc. All rights reserved.
Parent Flyer may be reproduced for noncommercial use.

Parent Flyer

Dear Parents,

We are learning about community helpers. Try doing the following activities to reinforce your child's understanding of the dentist and dental hygiene.

Happy Tooth, Sad Tooth Puppet

Cut a tooth shape out of stiff white paper. Let your child draw a happy face on one side of the tooth and a sad face on the other side. Attach a craft stick to the tooth shape for a handle. Help your child tear or cut pictures of foods out of magazines and place them in a pile. Hold up the pictures one at a time. Ask your child to show you the happy tooth puppet face if the food item is low in sugar or the sad tooth face if the food is high in sugar.

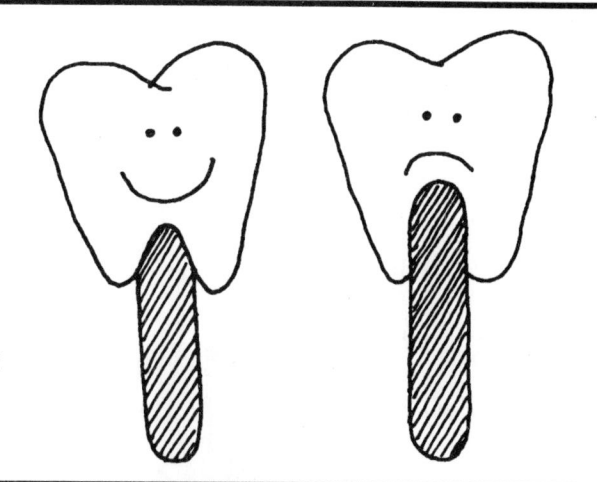

This Is the Way

Talk with your child about the proper way to brush and floss teeth. Then together, sing the following song and act out the movements described.

Sung to: "The Mulberry Bush"

This is the way we brush our teeth,
Brush our teeth, brush our teeth,
This is the way we brush our teeth,
So early in the morning.

This is the way we floss our teeth,
Floss our teeth, floss our teeth,
This is the way we floss our teeth,
So early in the morning.

Adapted Traditional

Going to the Dentist
Sung to: "She'll Be Coming Round the Mountain"

Going to the dentist, yes we are,
Going to the dentist, yes we are.
Be sure to take good care
Of our teeth inside there.
   (Point to mouth.)
Going to the dentist, yes we are.

Kristine Wagoner

Copyright ©1992 Warren Publishing House, Inc. All rights reserved.
Parent Flyer may be reproduced for noncommercial use.

Parent Flyer

Dear Parents,

We are learning about community helpers. Try doing the following activities to help reinforce your child's understanding of the mail carrier and the post office.

Milk Carton Mailbox

Help your child make a mailbox for his or her room. Wash and dry a half-gallon milk carton and cut off the top. Cover the outside of the carton with light-colored construction paper. Write your address on the side of the carton and use a brass paper fastener to attach a small flag shape cut from stiff red paper. Let your child add decorations as desired. Periodically, slip cards, notes and other "mail" into the mailbox for your child to discover.

Mail Carrier Song
Sung to: "My Bonnie Lies Over the Ocean"

I get to sort the mail,
Then carry it to your home.
The mail comes from all over,
Like New York, Paris and Rome.
Mail, mail, mail, mail,
I love to deliver the mail, mail, mail.
Mail, mail, mail, mail,
I love to deliver the mail.

Jean Warren

What's in the Mail
Sung to: "Three Blind Mice"

What's in the mail? What's in the mail?
I just can't wait to see.
There could be a postcard from far away,
There could be a letter from friends my age,
There could be a card saying happy birthday.
Oh, what's in the mail?

Diane Thom

Postcards

Use two large index cards to make postcards with your child. Visit the post office and mail the cards to each other at your address. Then watch together at home for the mail carrier to deliver your special mail.

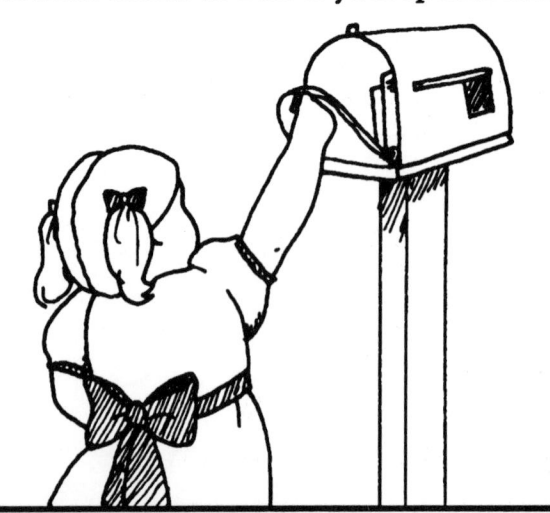

Copyright ©1992 Warren Publishing House, Inc. All rights reserved.
Parent Flyer may be reproduced for noncommercial use.

Parent Flyer

Dear Parents,

We are learning about community helpers. Try doing the following activities to help reinforce your child's understanding of the veterinarian and proper pet care.

Pet Care

If your family has a pet, talk with your child about the things you must do for it every day (give it food, water, exercise, etc.). Make a chart listing those tasks and let your child help decorate it. Display the chart in an appropriate place. Each day, check off the tasks on the chart with your child as you complete them together.

Variation: Provide your child with a toy animal "pet." Encourage your child to show you how he or she feeds the pet, grooms it, exercises it and plays with it.

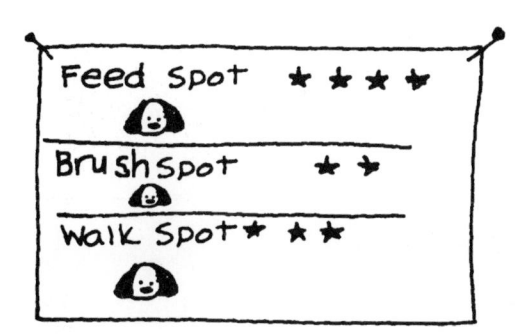

Pet Store Visit

Visit a pet store with your child. Talk about the different animals and pet supplies that are on display. Ask a clerk to explain the kinds of care that the animals need every day. Which pets require the most care? The least care?

I'm a Vet
Sung to: "Oh, My Darling Clementine"

I'm a vet, I'm a vet,
I'm a veterinarian.
I take care of the animals,
And I treat them one by one.

I give shots, I set legs,
And sometimes I operate.
I take care of the animals,
'Cause I think they are just great.

Bring your dogs, bring your cats,
Bring your hamsters one by one.
I take care of the animals,
I'm a veterinarian.

Repeat, letting your child substitute other animal names for *dogs, cats* and *hamsters*.

Jean Warren

Copyright ©1992 Warren Publishing House, Inc. All rights reserved.
Parent Flyer may be reproduced for noncommercial use.

Community Helpers Contributors

Ideas in this chapter were contributed by:

Valerie Bielsker, Lenexa, KS
Janice Bodenstedt, Jackson, MI
Sue Brown, Louisville, KY
Judith Taylor Burtchet, El Dorado, KS
Frank Dally, Ankeny, IA
Leora Grecian, San Bernadino, CA
Cathy B. Griffin, Plainsboro, NJ
Judy Hall, Wytheville, VA
Peggy Hanley, St. Joseph, MI
Nancy J. Heimark, Grand Forks, ND
Joan Hunter, Elbridge, NY
Ellen Javernick, Loveland, CO
Neoma Kreuter, Ontario, CA
Susan A. Miller, Kutztown, PA
Susan Peters, Upland, CA
Beverly Qualheim, Marquette, MI
Deborah Roessel, Flemington, NJ
Debbie Scofield, Niceville, FL
Betty Silkunas, Lansdale, PA
Diane Thom, Maple Valley, WA
Bobby Lee Wagman, Milton, WI
Kristine Wagoner, Puyallup, WA
Anne Lemay Zipf, Metuchen, NJ

Learning About

WELCOME TO THE ZOO

SOME PLACES WE GO

Getting There

Car Tracks Mural

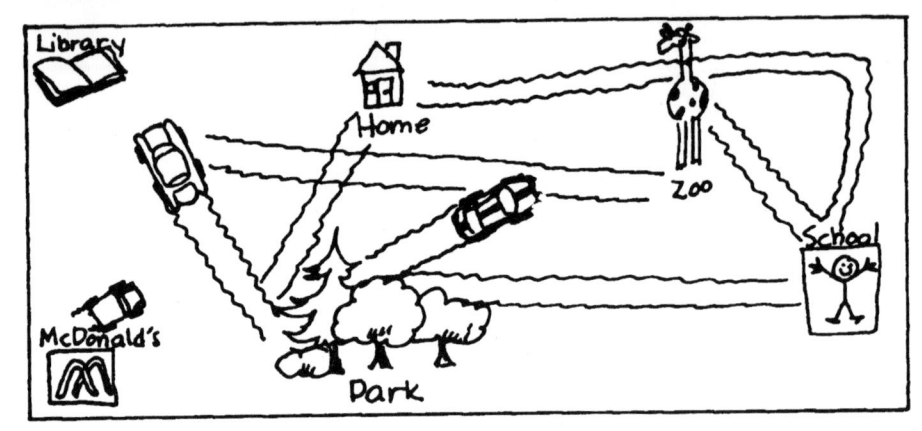

On a piece of butcher paper, draw simple pictures at random of three or four familiar places (your teaching center, a park, a library, the zoo, etc.). Tape the paper to a tabletop or the floor. Pour different colors of tempera paint into shallow containers. Let the children dip the wheels of toy cars into the paint and drive the cars from one place to another on the butcher paper any way they wish. When the paint has dried, display the Car Tracks Mural on a wall or a bulletin board.

Pretend Bus Trip

Cut a large bus shape from heavy brown cardboard or butcher paper. Let the children help color the shape with felt-tip markers. Cut a large window out of the bus shape and cover it with clear self-stick paper, if desired. Line up several child-size chairs for bus seats. Stand the bus shape next to the chairs and tape it securely in place. Let the children sit in the chairs and decide where they want to go on their pretend bus trip. Have them look out the window and talk about the things they see as they ride along.

Variation: Create a "bus" by lining up a long row of chairs. Choose one child to sit at the front and be the driver. Let the driver tell where the bus is going while the passengers point out things they see on the way.

Some Places We Go

All Around the Town

Sung to: "Ten Little Indians"

Hop aboard my little red car,
Hop aboard my little red car,
Hop aboard my little red car,
Let's ride around the town.

Round and around and around we go,
Round and around and around we go,
Round and around and around we go,
All around the town.

Additional verses: Hop aboard my big long bus; Hop aboard my big blue truck; Hop aboard my black and white taxi; etc.

Jean Warren

Taxi Cab Game

Give each child several green construction-paper "dollars." Make taxis by putting two chairs together, one behind the other. Let half of the children pretend to be cabbies and sit in the front chairs. Have the rest of the children pretend to be passengers. Explain that to take a taxi ride a passenger must give a designated number of dollars to a cabbie before sitting down in the back seat of the cab. Let the passengers move from cab to cab and ride to different imaginary destinations. Then have the cabbies and the passengers trade places.

Some Places We Go

Library

Picture Books

Make a blank book for each child by stapling sheets of white paper together with a colored construction-paper cover. Choose a theme such as toys. Write "My Toy Book" and a child's name on each book cover. Have the children look through magazines and catalogs to find pictures of toys. Then have them tear or cut out the pictures and glue them in their books. (Let younger children choose from precut pictures that have been placed in a box.) As the children "read" their books to you, write their comments on their book pages, if desired.

Variation: Let each child choose the kind of picture book that he or she would like to make.

We Love Books

Sung to: "Three Blind Mice"

We love books, we love books,
All kinds of books, all kinds of books.
Let's go right now to the library,
It's filled with books we can read for free.
They're waiting there for you and me.
We love books.

Jean Warren

Some Places We Go

Library

Library Play Center

Set up a play library in a corner of your room. Arrange books on shelves and provide a few chairs or pillows. Let the children take turns being the librarian and standing at a library desk. Give each child a pretend library card made from posterboard. When the children find books that they want to check out, have them take the books to the librarian, show their library cards and let the librarian pretend to stamp their books (or run them through the computer). When they finish their reading, have the children return their books to the desk for the librarian to put back on the shelves.

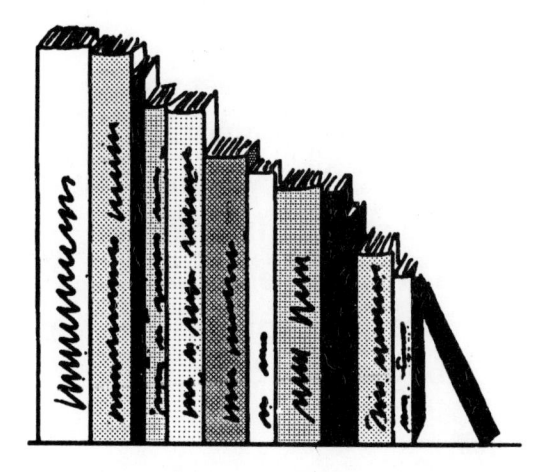

Book Shelving Game

Set out various sizes of picture books. Let the children arrange the books on a bookshelf from tallest to shortest. Then have them count the number of books on the shelf.

Variation: Attach removable circle stickers in different colors to the spines of the books (red for storybooks, blue for animal books, etc.). Let the children arrange the books on the shelf by color.

Some Places We Go

Zoo

Stand-up Zoo Animals

Cut different zoo animal shapes out of stiff paper. Cut the legs off each shape. Let the children choose the animal shapes they want and color them on both sides with crayons or felt-tip markers. Have them add facial features and other details as desired. For each animal shape, provide two wooden spring-type clothespins. Let the children color the clothespins and clip them to their animal shapes for legs.

Going to the Zoo
Sung to: "Yankee Doodle"

If you're going to the zoo,
Remember who will meet you.
Tigers, zebras, porcupines,
And monkeys, they will greet you.
Next you'll see the king of all,
And lion is his name.
The giraffes and elephants
Will all be glad you came.

Judy Hall

Some Places We Go

Play Zoo

Provide the children with toy zoo animals. Let them make a "natural-habitat" zoo for the animals on butcher paper that has been taped to the floor. Have them paint grassy areas green, water areas blue and sandy areas brown. If desired, let them sprinkle some sand on the brown paint while it is still wet. Talk about which environment is best for each animal. Then let the children use natural materials, such as rocks, twigs, leaves, grass and wood scraps, to create separate living areas for the animals.

Zoo Animal Charades

Have the children sit with you in a group. Show pictures of different zoo animals and discuss their characteristics. Then whisper the name of one of the zoo animals in a child's ear. Have the child stand in front of the group and act out the animal's movements while the other children try to guess what the animal is. Let the first child to guess correctly have the next turn.

Some Places We Go

School

School Bus Mural

Cut a long school bus shape out of butcher paper. Draw as many windows on the bus shape as there are children in your group. Let the children help paint the bus shape yellow. Add black wheels and other details as desired. Let the children draw self-portraits on separate pieces of construction paper. Cut the windows out of the bus shape and glue a self-portrait in each window opening. Then hang the school bus shape on a wall or a bulletin board.

School Play Center

Set up a pretend school area in a corner of your room. Include desks for a teacher and several students. Supply your play center with school materials such as a chalkboard, a memo board, learning games, storybooks, pretend worksheets, pencils, paper and crayons. Let the children take turns being the teacher and helping the students do pretend reading, writing and math activities. Let the teacher also check attendance lists, "read" messages from the principal and "write" pretend notes to send home to parents.

Some Places We Go

Off to School We Go

Sung to: "The Farmer in the Dell"

Off to school we go,
It's off to school we go.
We'll take our lunch and ride the bus,
With everyone we know.

Off to school we go,
It's off to school we go.
We'll learn our *ABC*'s and more,
With everyone we know.

Judy Hall

Alphabet Block Match

Print letters or simple words on index cards. Place the cards and a set of alphabet blocks on a table. Let the children select cards and find alphabet blocks that match the letters on the cards.

Variation: Print the children's names on large index cards. Let the children match the alphabet blocks to the letters in their names.

Park

Park Rubbings

Go on a walk with the children to a nearby park. Take along a shopping bag containing old crayons and pieces of plain newsprint or other lightweight paper. As you walk through the park, let the children experiment with making rubbings of different textured surfaces (tree trunks, stones, leaves, cement pathways, metal grillwork, etc.). When you return to your room, display the rubbings and encourage the children to talk about how they made them.

Play Park

Let the children make a play park for small plastic people and animals. Give them an old green bedspread (or piece of fabric) to arrange on the floor for a base. Secure it with tape, if desired. Let the children make trees for their park by sticking twigs into balls of playdough or modeling clay. For a pond, give them an oval shape cut from blue posterboard and let them cover it with clear plastic wrap, if desired. Encourage the children to add other items such as rocks, wood block "buildings" and a miniature sandbox.

Some Places We Go

Park Activity Sorting Game

Cut pictures from magazines of people engaged in various activities. Include pictures of things that people might do in a park (jogging, picnicking, playing on swings, wading in a pool, observing birds, etc.). Also include pictures of things that people normally do not do in a park (baking cookies, vacuuming, brushing teeth, sleeping in a bed, using a computer, etc.). Mount the pictures on separate pieces of construction paper and place them in a pile. Let the children take turns sorting the pictures into two groups: those that show activities people do in a park and those that show activities people don't do in a park.

We're Off to the Park Today

Sung to: "The Farmer in the Dell"

We're off to the park today,
We're off to the park today.
Heigh-ho, away we go,
We're off to the park today.

We'll play on the swings today,
We'll play on the swings today.
Heigh-ho, away we go,
We'll play on the swings today.

Additional verses: We'll fly our kites today; We'll have a picnic today; We'll run and hide today; We'll feed the ducks today; etc.

Jean Warren

Some Places We Go

Parent Flyer

Dear Parents,

We have been learning about some of the places we visit in our community. Try doing the following activities to help your child learn more about traveling around town and what we can see as we travel.

Bus Ride

Take your child on a short bus ride in your neighborhood. If possible, let your child deposit his or her own fare in the coin box. Along the way, have your child look for familiar landmarks such as stores, restaurants or parks. Also ask him or her to look for and count stop signs or traffic lights. When it's time to get off the bus, let your child pull the cord to signal the driver to stop.

I Love to Ride in a Car

Sung to: "My Bonnie Lies Over the Ocean"

I love to ride in a car,
Now I will tell you why.
I love to look out the window,
And watch the cars go by.
Cars, cars, cars, cars,
And watch the cars go by, go by,
Cars, cars, cars, cars,
And watch the cars go by

Repeat, letting your child name other things that he or she likes to watch go by while riding in a car.

Jean Warren

Travel Games

When traveling around town with your child, play games like these:

- Call out a color and a type of vehicle such as "blue station wagon." See who can spot the first one.

- Select a category of items to count such as supermarkets, vans or billboards. See who can count the highest number of items in a period of 5 or 10 minutes.

Copyright ©1992 Warren Publishing House, Inc. All rights reserved.
Parent Flyer may be reproduced for noncommercial use.

Parent Flyer

Dear Parents,

We have been learning about some of the public places that are found in many towns. Below is a song about those places that you can sing with your child.

Let's Go
Sung to: "The Mulberry Bush"

Let's go in the car today,
Car today, car today,
Let's go in the car today,
To see what we can see.

Let's go to the zoo today,
Zoo today, zoo today,
Let's go to the zoo today,
To watch the animals play.

Let's go to the school today,
School today, school today,
Let's go to the school today,
To watch the children learn.

Let's go to the library today,
Library today, library today,
Let's go to the library today,
To look at all the books.

Let's go to the park today,
Park today, park today,
Let's go to the park today,
To see the grass and trees.

Make up new verses about other places that you and your child like to visit.

Gayle Bittinger

Copyright ©1992 Warren Publishing House, Inc. All rights reserved.
Parent Flyer may be reproduced for noncommercial use.

Some Places We Go Contributors

Ideas in this chapter were contributed by:

Sue Brown, Louisville, KY
Judy Hall, Wytheville, VA
Neoma Kreuter, Ontario, CA
Susan M. Paprocki, Northbrook, IL

Totline® Newsletter

Activities, songs and new ideas to use right now are waiting for you in every issue!

Each issue puts the fun into teaching with 32 pages of challenging and creative activities for young children. Included are open-ended art activities, learning games, music, language and science activities plus 8 reproducible pattern pages.

Published bi-monthly.

Sample issue - $2.00

Super Snack News

Nutritious snack ideas, related songs, rhymes and activities

- Teach young children health and nutrition through fun and creative activities.
- Use as a handout to involve parents in their children's education.
- Promote quality child care in the community with these handouts.
- Includes nutritious sugarless snacks, health tidbits, and developmentally appropriate activities.
- Includes CACFP information for most snacks.

Sample issue - $2.00

With each subscription you are given the right to:

Make up to: **200 COPIES** per issue

Warren Publishing House, Inc. • P.O. Box 2250, Dept. Z • Everett, WA 98203

Totline® Books

PIGGYBACK® SONG SERIES

Piggyback® Songs

More Piggyback® Songs

Piggyback® Songs for Infants & Toddlers

Piggyback® Songs in Praise of God

Piggyback® Songs in Praise of Jesus

Holiday Piggyback® Songs

Animal Piggyback® Songs

Piggyback® Songs for School

Piggyback® Songs to Sign

1•2•3 SERIES

1•2•3 Art

1•2•3 Games

1•2•3 Colors

1•2•3 Puppets

1•2•3 Murals

1•2•3 Books

1•2•3 Reading & Writing

1•2•3 Rhymes, Stories & Songs

1•2•3 Math

1•2•3 Science

EXPLORING SERIES

Exploring Sand

Exploring Water

Exploring Wood

CELEBRATION SERIES

Small World Celebrations

Special Day Celebrations

Yankee Doodle Birthday Celebrations

Great Big Holiday Celebrations

CUT & TELL SERIES

Scissor Stories for Fall

Scissor Stories for Winter

Scissor Stories for Spring

TEACHING TALE SERIES

Teeny-Tiny Folktales

Short-Short Stories

Mini-Mini Musicals

THEME-A-SAURUS® SERIES

Theme-A-Saurus®

Theme-A-Saurus® II

Toddler Theme-A-Saurus®

Alphabet Theme-A-Saurus®

Nursery Rhyme Theme-A-Saurus®

Storytime Theme-A-Saurus®

TAKE-HOME SERIES

Alphabet & Number Rhymes

Color, Shape & Season Rhymes

Object Rhymes

Animal Rhymes

LEARNING & CARING ABOUT SERIES

Our World

Our Selves

Our Town

MIX & MATCH PATTERNS

Animal Patterns

Everyday Patterns

Holiday Patterns

Nature Patterns

ABC SERIES

ABC Space

ABC Farm

ABC Zoo

ABC Circus

1001 SERIES

1001 Teaching Props

OTHER

Super Snacks

Celebrating Childhood

Home Activity Booklet

23 Hands-On Workshops

Totline books are available at school supply stores and parent/teacher stores, or write for our free catalog.

Warren Publishing House, Inc. • P.O. Box 2250, Dept. B • Everett, WA 98203